See, I Can Read Too!

Written by
Tameka Rogers-Colbert

Illustrated by
Wilson Williams, Jr.

Hope of Visions Publishing

See, I Can Read Too!
Text copyright © 2011 Tameka Rogers-Cobert
Illustrations copyright © 2011 Wilson Williams, Jr.

All rights reserved. No part of this book may be reproduced, copied, stored or transmitted in any form or by any means-graphic, electronic, or mechanical, including photocopying, recording, or information storage and retrieval systems without the prior written permission of Tameka Rogers-Colbert or Hope of Vision Publishing except where permitted by law.

Hope of Vision Publishing a division of HOV, LLC
www.Hopeofvisionpublishing.com or www.Hovpub.com
hopeofvision@gmail.com

Contact the Author:
info@seeicanreadtoo.com
Visit us at: www.seeicanreadtoo.com
"Transforming Your Child Through the Power of Reading"
TRC Publications, LLC
P.O. Box 644
Tifton, GA 31793-0644

Book Design and Illustrations by: Wilson Williams, Jr.
visit us at: www.doublewillustrations.com

For more information about special discounts for bulk purchases, please contact Tameka Rogers-Colbert or Hope of Vision Publishing.

Library of Congress Number: 2010928418
ISBN: 978-0-9753795-6-1
Printed in the United States of America

A note on the art; All artwork was created digitally using Photoshop.

This book is lovingly dedicated
to my two children,
Jada and Destin
And to my Mother
Earnestine Williams-Rogers

Special Acknowledgement

To Ms. Shirley Cutts, Tifton, Georgia

*Thanks for inspiring me as a young child
to write and for encouraging me
to articulate my thoughts
into expressive writing.*

-T.R.C.

For my Mother,
without you none of this
would be possible
-W.W.JR.

Tasha McKenzie laid sound asleep, upon her wooden bed.

Her Mother gazed at her smiling, as she bent over and kissed her on the forehead.

Outside the wind was blowing, it was nice, but rather cool.

Tasha heard the voice of her Mother say,

"Wake up!
It's time to go to school!"

Tasha jumped up with joy and got dressed. Oh-was she ready for the first grade!

When Tasha arrived at school, everyone seemed nice and very cool. Except a few kids in her class who were often, awfully rude!

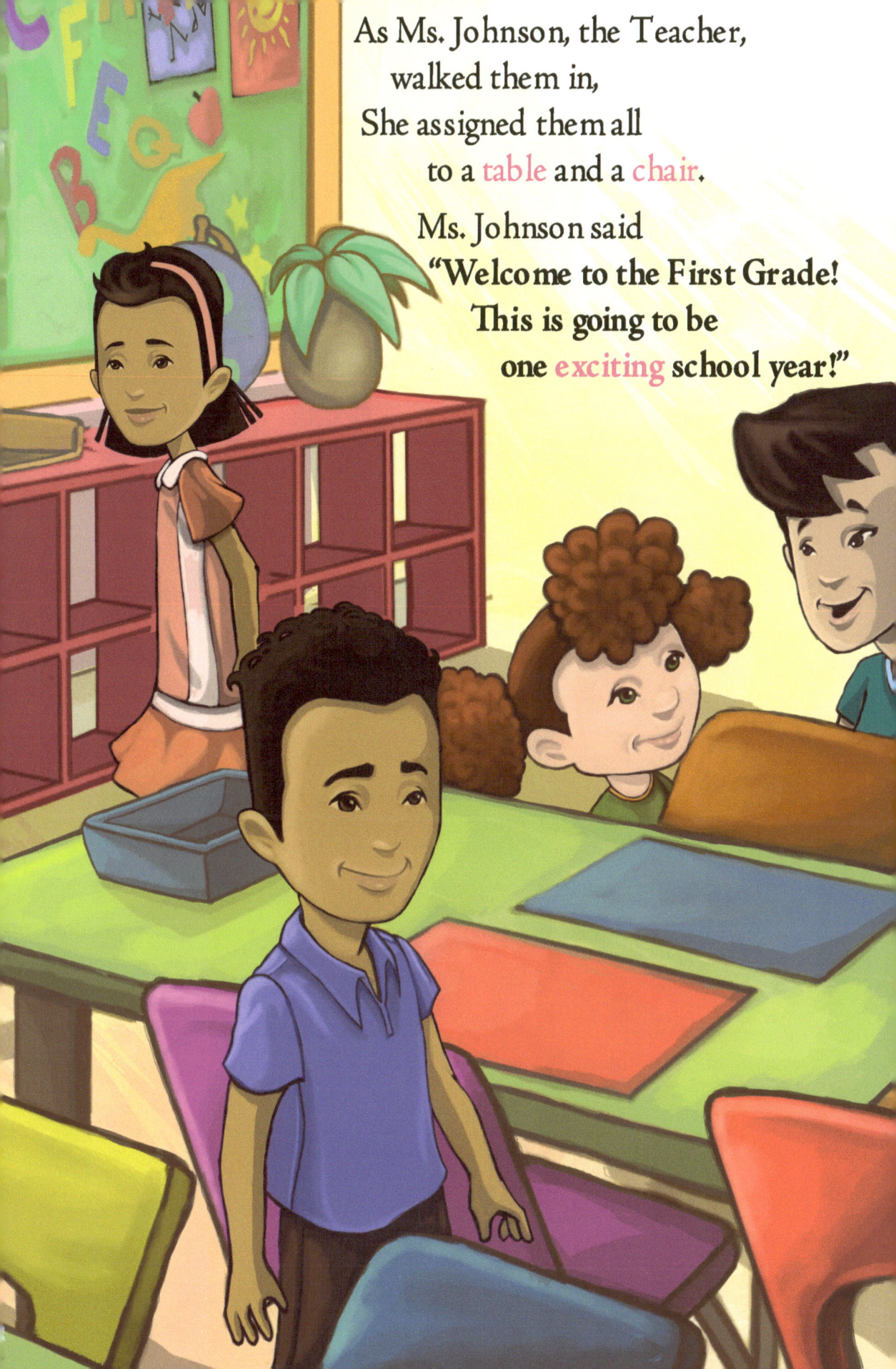

Tasha was so excited! But what she didn't understand was this year would be challenging for her, one that she'd wish would end.

As days went by her teacher introduced the **vowels**, A, E, I, O and U, but Tasha had a hard time comprehending the sounds of each letter, **she didn't know what to do.**

Her classmates were grasping and blending the sounds They did this each and every day, but when the teacher asked Tasha if she understood, she remained silent and confused not knowing what to say.

Some of her classmates would tease her daily because she was not catching on. Tasha felt bad, and she didn't like school anymore, all she wanted to do was stay home.

Then one day, as Tasha's Mom passed her room, She heard sounds of *sighing*.

As her Mother slowly opened the door, she saw little Tasha, lying on her bed, *crying*.

"Well I'm going to help you," said her Mama, "and teach you how to master this skill! So baby, dry your eyes! Stop the crying! Because your Mama is here!"

Tasha's Mama read to her daily, as they walked around in the yard.

She taught her how to blend letters into words, and how to memorize them by using flash cards.

As days went by, Ms. Johnson noticed
Tasha was finally catching on.
Tasha would purposely
remain silent however,
allowing her classmates
to carry on.

Two months later it was "Show and Tell" at Harper Elementary School.

Tasha knew exactly what she wanted to bring.

She knew just what to do!

As her classmates showed and told of their favorite toys, Tasha sat back and looked.

Tasha did not bring a toy to "Show and Tell" Tasha brought a book!

When Tasha's turn finally came,
she knew that it was her time to shine.
What she desired to "Show and Tell"
was to read her book aloud
for the first time!

Tasha approached the front of the class.

Her classmates watched with curious eyes.

They had no idea what they were about to witness.

They were all in for a huge surprise!

Tasha stood with confidence
and read her entire book,
with such a great sound!

Her classmates were so amazed;
their mouths almost hit the ground!

Everyone clapped and shouted for Tasha,
As they let out their
Aaahh's and Ooohh's
Tasha, with a big smile, turned and said,

"See, I can READ too!"

Tameka Rogers-Colbert attains a fervent passion for educational advancement amalgamated with linguistics and the foundations of literature. Fueling her aspiration was the literary apt and success of her daughter, Jada's ability to read at the age of 3 using flashcards.

Pressing beyond the realm of her immediate environment, Tameka ventured to assist other children by founding a non-profit organization, T.Colbert Youth Outreach & Scholarship Organization, Inc. As President, Tameka designed the organization to unlock doors of opportunity for youth through outreach and scholarship programs.

A native resident of Tifton, Georgia, Tameka ignited her life's ardor of children's literature in her book, *See, I Can Read Too!* Tameka's sincere desire to use her children's books to literate and motivate children to read in a fun-filled manner, while inspiring children to develop an inner confidence and to stimulate parental involvement into their child's reading experience.

The muse for *See, I Can Read Too!* was conceived in the hallowed halls and classrooms of Harper Elementary School in Riverdale, Georgia. This birthing place spawned Tameka's intrinsic zeal to motivate youth about education.

Contact the Author
info@seeicanreadtoo.com

Visit the site at
www.seeicanreadtoo.com

"Transforming Your Child Through The Power of Reading"

www.ingramcontent.com/pod-product-compliance
Lightning Source LLC
Chambersburg PA
CBHW041119300426
44112CB00002B/36